60
SUPER
SIMPLE
SCIENCE
EXPERIMENTS

By Q. L. Pearce

Illustrated by Leo Abbett

LOWELL HOUSE JUVENILE

LOS ANGELES

NTC/Contemporary Publishing Group

NOTE TO THE READER:

Many of the experiments in *60 Super Simple Science Experiments* may require the use of a measuring cup, measuring spoons, a ruler, or a clock. These items are not listed under What You'll Need, unless they are needed for a specific purpose other than measuring.

Published by Lowell House
A division of NTC/Contemporary Publishing Group, Inc., 4255 West Touhy Avenue,
Lincolnwood (Chicago), Illinois 60646-1975 U.S.A.

Managing Director and Publisher: Jack Artenstein
Director of Publishing Services: Rena Copperman
Editorial Director, Juvenile: Brenda Pope-Ostrow
Director of Juvenile Development: Amy Downing
Director of Art Production: Bret Perry
Project Editor: Joanna Siebert
Typesetter: Treesha Runnells

Lowell House books can be purchased at special discounts when ordered in bulk for premiums and special sales.
Please contact Customer Service at:
NTC/Contemporary
4255 W. Touhy Avenue
Lincolnwood, IL 60646-1975
1-800-323-4900

Printed and bound in the United States of America

Library of Congress Catalog Card Number: 98-66659

ISBN: 1-56565-688-1

10 9 8 7 6 5 4 3

CONTENTS

SHIVER
AND STEAM

Matter is any physical thing that takes up space. Try this experiment with water to see the three different states of matter. (You'll need to know how to use a microwave oven for this experiment.)

WHAT YOU'LL NEED
• **two ice cubes** • **zip-top sandwich bag** • **microwave-safe dish** • **microwave oven**

DIRECTIONS

❶ Put the ice cubes in the sandwich bag, then seal it. Place the bag on a microwave-safe dish and set it in the microwave.

❷ Turn the microwave on at full power for one minute and watch as the ice cubes melt and become liquid. You may have to run it for an additional 30 seconds to melt all the ice.

❸ Now run the microwave for another 30 seconds. What happens to the bag? Let the bag cool completely before removing it from the microwave.

WHAT HAPPENED?

All matter is made up of tiny units called molecules. Matter can take three different forms—solid, liquid, or gas. When a substance is in its solid state, the molecules are slow-moving and packed closely together. Ice is the solid state of water. In this experiment you add energy by heating the ice in the microwave. The molecules begin to move faster and farther apart until the water reaches a liquid state. When you continue to heat the liquid, the molecules move even faster and farther apart to become water vapor, which is a gas. The expanding water vapor causes the bag to puff up.

SURPRISING RISING BALL

How does matter respond to its environment? This experiment demonstrates a characteristic, or property, of matter.

WHAT YOU'LL NEED

• 2 cups uncooked rice • quart jar with lid • large marble or Ping-Pong ball

DIRECTIONS

1 Pour the rice into the jar.

2 Place the marble or Ping-Pong ball on top of the rice. Fasten the lid onto the jar, then turn the jar over.

3 Using one hand, shake the jar hard from side to side. As you are shaking it, the marble or ball will rise to the surface.

WHAT HAPPENED?

The rice may fill part of the jar, but something else is between each grain—empty space. When you shake the jar, the rice grains tumble over each other, filling in the empty spaces. The marble or ball is too big to fill in any of these spaces, so it moves upward. This experiment demonstrates a property of matter: No two objects can occupy the same place at the same time.

UPS AND DOWNS

Have you ever taken a sip of soda and felt a tickle at the end of your nose? That's caused by tiny bubbles of carbon dioxide, a gas, which gives soda its fizz. Those bubbles can do more, too. Try this and learn about some properties of gas.

WHAT YOU'LL NEED

• **glass pint jar** • **unopened bottle of club soda** • **10 raisins**

DIRECTIONS

1 Fill the jar with club soda.

2 Add the raisins, one at a time, to the club soda, and watch what happens. The raisins will rise, then fall, then eventually rise again.

WHAT HAPPENED?

Club soda fizzes because it is filled with carbon dioxide gas. The gas bubbles rise because they are lighter than the liquid they are in. In this experiment the bubbles cling to the raisins and carry them to the surface. When the bubbles break, the raisins sink, until new bubbles attach to the raisins and carry them up again.

DANCING COIN

Here's a way to make a coin jump without even touching it. It isn't magic, it's a demonstration of the effect of gas expansion.

WHAT YOU'LL NEED

• empty 2-liter soda bottle with no cap • freezer • quarter • water

DIRECTIONS

1 Put the empty, open soda bottle in the freezer for about 10 minutes.

2 Dip the quarter in water.

3 Take the bottle out of the freezer and set it on a flat surface in a sunny spot. Quickly cover the open mouth of the bottle with the wet coin. The coin will soon start to tap up and down. As long as the coin is centered over the opening of the bottle, the tapping will continue.

WHAT HAPPENED?

By putting the bottle in the freezer, you chill the air that is inside the bottle. The cold air contracts, which means it takes up less space. When you take the bottle out of the freezer, the air inside warms and expands but is trapped by the wet coin. The wetness helps to create a seal that keeps the air inside the bottle. As the air slowly pushes upward, it builds up enough pressure to lift the coin and escape in a short burst. The pressure must build again before another burst of air can escape. The coin jumps slightly each time the air escapes.

WHERE DID
IT GO?

You can make matter appear to disappear right before your eyes. It isn't really gone, though. What seems like sleight of hand is really an example of a solution.

WHAT YOU'LL NEED

• 1¼ cups water at room temperature • glass pint jar • marking pen
• masking tape (optional) • spoon • ¼ cup sugar

DIRECTIONS

❶ Pour ¼ cup water into the jar. Draw a line to mark the water level and label it ¼. If your pen won't work on glass, write on a piece of masking tape and put it on the jar at the right water level. Add another ¼ cup water and mark it ½. Add one more ¼ cup water and label it ¾.

❷ Empty the contents of the jar into the sink. Refill the jar with water to the ½ cup mark.

❸ With a spoon, stir ¼ cup sugar into the water and check the level of the fluid. Do ½ cup water and ¼ cup sugar equal ¾ cup water?

| ¼ water | + | ¼ water | + | ¼ water | ? = | ¼ water | + | ¼ water | + | ¼ sugar |

WHAT HAPPENED?

In a liquid state, water molecules have plenty of spaces in between them. Many of the sugar molecules simply fill up these spaces without making much of a change in the water level. When the sugar dissolves, or fills in the spaces between the water molecules, a solution is formed. The sugar serves as a solute (the material that dissolves), and the water serves as a solvent (what the material dissolves in).

TO SPILL OR NOT TO SPILL

Surprise your friends at lunchtime with this experiment. Just be sure to move fast as you demonstrate the properties of polymers, or your performance will be all wet!

WHAT YOU'LL NEED

• zip-top sandwich bag • water • sharpened pencil

DIRECTIONS

❶ Fill the plastic bag with water and seal it.

❷ Hold the bag in front of you. As quickly as you can, stab the pencil through one side of the bag and out the other (speed is very important).

WHAT HAPPENED?

Some types of molecules form long chains called polymers. Some polymers are found in natural substances, such as rubber and starch, whereas others are in manufactured goods, such as most plastics. Polyethylene (a type of plastic made from polymers) has a unique property—it shrinks when ripped or when a hole is stabbed in it. When you stab the pencil through the plastic bag, it tightens around the pencil to seal the hole.

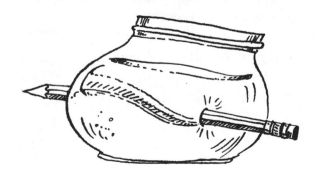

RIPPLING
RAINBOW

Turn plain water into a cherry-red liquid without even stirring it. There's no confusion—it's diffusion!

WHAT YOU'LL NEED
• glass pint jar • water • red food coloring

DIRECTIONS

❶ Fill the jar almost to the top with water.

❷ Set the jar on a flat surface and add 10 drops of red food coloring.

❸ Without disturbing the jar, note what happens during the next 15 minutes. The coloring will slowly swirl and spread all by itself.

WHAT HAPPENED?

Molecules, in any state of matter, are always moving. Molecules move faster in liquids than they do in solids, and they move even faster in gases. In this experiment you can't see the molecules, but you can see what happens when food coloring molecules are struck by water molecules. The process by which solids, liquids, or gases mix together is called diffusion. Because of diffusion, the food coloring spreads through the water on its own, turning the liquid bright red.

Something Extra

Diffusion can also take place in air, which is a gas. Try this with a friend. Stand against a wall on one side of a room, and have your friend stand against the opposite wall. Spray some cologne or room deodorizer into the air. Time how long it takes until your friend detects the scent. Do you think the process of diffusion happens more quickly in air than in water?

8

MAGIC
MUD

Some substances don't dissolve in water; instead, they do something very interesting. Try the experiment below to create a suspension.

WHAT YOU'LL NEED

• 4-ounce bottle of white glue • 1½ cups distilled water • two medium glass bowls • two spoons • 1 teaspoon borax powder

DIRECTIONS

1 Mix the entire bottle of glue and ½ cup distilled water in one bowl. Stir with a spoon.

2 Pour 1 cup distilled water and 1 teaspoon borax powder into the second bowl. Stir well with the second spoon.

3 Pour the glue mixture into the borax mixture and stir until you have a thick blob.

4 Lift the mixture out of the bowl and knead it with your hands until it feels like dough. Try ripping it, pulling it apart slowly, and even bouncing it.

WHAT HAPPENED?

The white glue is made up of polymers that become suspended in water. Before you mix the glue with anything else, these polymers tend to slide over each other. Adding borax to the glue causes the polymers to stop moving and form a sort of meshwork instead. The result is a concentrated suspension—liquid water with lots of tiny solid particles (in this case, the polymers) suspended in it. The solid particles do not fit into the spaces between the water molecules, so they can't dissolve in the liquid.

9

G O B S
O F G O O

Have you ever heard of the saying "Go with the flow"? Learn what that really means by experimenting with a non-Newtonian fluid.

WHAT YOU'LL NEED
• cornstarch • small bowl • water • spoon

DIRECTIONS

1 Put ¼ cup cornstarch in the bowl.

2 Add 6 teaspoons water, then stir. If it is too hard to stir, add a little more water. If the mixture gets too watery, add more cornstarch. The mixture should be fluid but very hard to mix. It should feel like thick mud.

3 When you think that you have the right consistency, scoop out a handful and quickly roll it back and forth between the palms of your hands. It will become firm.

4 Stop rolling and hold the mixture in your hand over the bowl. The goo will drip from your fingers. When you are finished with the experiment, let the mixture become firm, then put it in the trash. Do not throw it down the sink, as it can clog the drain.

WHAT HAPPENED?

The mixture you created is a non-Newtonian fluid. Fluids have a property called viscosity, or resistance to flow. Something with high viscosity, like honey, flows slowly. Something with low viscosity, like water, flows quickly. The scientist Sir Isaac Newton found that the viscosity of a fluid can be changed only by raising or lowering its temperature. Non-Newtonian fluids are an exception to that rule. The viscosity of these fluids can be changed by altering the temperature or by applying a force. In this experiment you apply a force to the fluid by rubbing it between your hands.

Something Extra

Here's another way to apply a force to the fluid in this experiment: Place the mixture in a shallow metal pan and bang the bottom of the pan sharply on a hard surface. The fluid will crack like a solid, then immediately flow together again.

CREEPING COLOR

A black line is a black line, right? This experiment using the pigments in ink shows that things aren't always what they seem.

WHAT YOU'LL NEED

• **scissors** • **coffee filter** • **water-soluble marking pen (black, green, or purple)**
• **water** • **glass quart jar** • **string** • **tape**

DIRECTIONS

1 Cut a strip from the coffee filter that is 1 inch wide and almost as tall as the jar. About 2 inches from one end of the strip, make a large dot with the marking pen.

2 Pour an inch of water into the jar.

3 Cut a piece of string, place it across the top of the open jar, and tape the ends to the jar. This will be the hanger for the filter strip.

❹ Place the filter strip inside the jar with the dot at the bottom end. The end of the paper should be in the water, but the dot should be about an inch above the water level. Tape the top of the strip to the string to hold it in place and watch what happens.

WHAT HAPPENED?

The water seeps up the paper through a process called capillary action. Water molecules move into the spaces between the fibers in the paper, then attract other water molecules to follow. As the water travels upward, it carries the ink along with it. The ink is made up of more than one color, or pigment. The colors slowly separate, allowing you to see the individual pigments that make up the ink. The weight of the chemicals used to produce the ink affects how far each pigment seeps up the paper—the lighter chemicals travel farthest.

BLOW
YOUR TOP!

Be a kitchen chemist—use baking soda and vinegar to create an amazing chemical reaction.

WHAT YOU'LL NEED

• spoon • ½ cup water • ½ cup vinegar • ¼ cup dishwashing liquid
• two glass pint jars • ¼ cup baking soda • medium-sized mixing bowl

DIRECTIONS

❶ Stir the water, vinegar, and dishwashing liquid together in one jar.

❷ Put the baking soda in the other jar. Place that jar in the bowl to catch any spillover.

❸ Pour the contents of the first jar into the second jar. Stir quickly and watch.

WHAT HAPPENED?

Baking soda is a base. Vinegar is an acid. When a base and an acid are combined, they create a chemical reaction. In a chemical reaction, molecules interact to create new molecules. Together, the baking soda and vinegar produce carbon dioxide gas.

Something Extra

Here's a way to really raise a reaction. In a 9- by 13-inch shallow baking dish, make a volcano from dirt, damp sand, or papier-mâché. Mold the shape with a pocket at the top to hold the jar of baking soda. Repeat the experiment above, and watch your volcano erupt!

ON THE HIGH SEAS

Have you ever noticed that oil and water don't mix? That's because they are immiscible (im-MIS-ih-bul) liquids. Check it out.

WHAT YOU'LL NEED
• water • empty soda bottle with cap, label removed (use 1-liter or 2-liter size)
• blue food coloring • bottle of baby oil

DIRECTIONS

❶ Pour water into the soda bottle until it is about three-quarters full. Add 5 to 10 drops of blue food coloring to the water and screw the cap on. Shake to mix.

❷ Unscrew the cap. Fill the bottle to the rim with baby oil, then put the cap back on.

❸ Hold the bottle on its side and gently tip it up and down. The colored water will look like the waves of the ocean.

WHAT HAPPENED?

This experiment is a demonstration of immiscible liquids—those liquids that are different from each other and will not mix together. As long as you move the bottle gently, the water and baby oil will stay separated.

Something Extra
Create a little sparkle by adding a teaspoon of glitter to the colored water in the bottle.

T I N Y
B U B B L E S

Why do some things float while others sink? Find out for yourself with this experiment about density.

WHAT YOU'LL NEED
• 1 cup rubbing alcohol • glass pint jar • ½ cup water
• 2 tablespoons cooking oil • empty 35mm film canister or small plastic container with cap
• food coloring, any color • eyedropper

DIRECTIONS

❶ Pour the rubbing alcohol into the jar, then add the water. The water will sink to the bottom of the jar.

❷ Pour the cooking oil into the film canister or small container. Add 5 drops of food coloring. Put the cap on, then shake hard to mix the oil and food coloring.

❸ Using an eyedropper, gently place drops of the oil mixture into the jar of water and rubbing alcohol.

4 If the drops sink, add more water to the jar, 1 tablespoon at a time, until they are suspended about midway in the fluid.

WHAT HAPPENED?

The density of an object or substance is the amount it weighs in relation to the amount of space it takes up. Water, alcohol, and oil have different densities. In this experiment the water sinks below the alcohol because it is heavier. The drops of oil also sink through the alcohol, but float on the water, because oil is heavier than alcohol and lighter than water. You may notice that the color slowly seeps out of the oil until the drops are clear. Oil and food coloring are immiscible liquids, or liquids that won't really mix together. They appear to be mixed when you shake the canister, but they eventually separate. Where does the color go? It spreads through the water.

HEAVY WATER

Which has greater density—salt water or fresh water? Here's a way to find out, but you may need a helper to get it right.

WHAT YOU'LL NEED
• two empty 2-liter soda bottles with no caps • water at room temperature
• 6 teaspoons salt • red food coloring • 3- by 5-inch card • duct tape

DIRECTIONS

❶ Fill both bottles with water.

❷ Add the salt and 10 drops of red food coloring to the first bottle only. Cover the top with your hand, then shake the bottle to mix the contents.

❸ Place the 3- by 5-inch card over the top of the first bottle. Hold the card in place with one hand and flip the bottle over.

❹ You may need help with this step. Balance the opening of the first bottle directly over the opening of the second bottle. When the bottles are as close to each other as possible, slip the card out. Adjust the bottles quickly so the water doesn't spill. Wrap duct tape around the necks of the bottles to prevent leaks.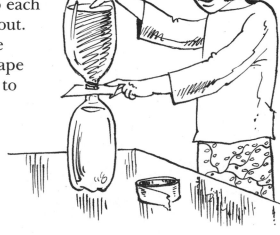

❺ Watch the bottles carefully. What happens to the colored water?

WHAT HAPPENED?

The volume, or amount, of water in each bottle is the same. If the density of water in each bottle was also the same—for instance, if the water in both bottles was room-temperature fresh water—then all the water would weigh the same and it would not shift around. In this experiment you use fresh water and salt water. Salt water is more dense than fresh water because of the salt, therefore it is also heavier. The colored salt water sinks to the bottom.

Something Extra

How could you adapt this experiment to test whether cold or warm water is more dense? Try out your idea to see if it works.

A CHILLY EXPERIENCE

The density of air varies with the temperature. Is it warmer near the floor or the ceiling in your home? Try this experiment, then think about the answer.

WHAT YOU'LL NEED
• seven ice cubes • 1 teaspoon salt • zip-top sandwich bag
• two pencils, sharpened • empty oatmeal box, lid removed
• outdoor thermometer • tape

DIRECTIONS

❶ Put the ice cubes and salt in the sandwich bag, then seal the bag.

❷ Use one pencil to make a thermometer-sized hole in the side of the oatmeal box about ½ inch from the bottom. Insert the thermometer about halfway in. Note the temperature.

❸ Set both pencils side by side across the top of the oatmeal box with a small space between them, then tape them in place. Balance the bag of ice and salt on top of the pencils.

❹ Wait 15 minutes, then read the temperature on the thermometer again.

WHAT HAPPENED?

Cold air is more dense than warm air, which makes it heavier. In this experiment the ice chills the air around the bag, then the cold air sinks to the bottom of the oatmeal box. That is why the temperature is lower when you check the thermometer the second time.

Something Extra

Here's a way to show that cold water sinks, too. Make an ice cube by freezing water mixed with food coloring. Put the ice cube in a glass of room-temperature water. As the ice melts, the cold, colored water will sink to the bottom of the glass to form a distinct layer.

BATTLE OF THE BULGE

Can a full glass of water become even fuller? Find out in this simple experiment.

WHAT YOU'LL NEED
• **clean, dry drinking glass** • **water** • **15 pennies**

DIRECTIONS

1 Fill the glass with water so that the surface of the water is even with the rim of the glass.

2 Lean down so that your eye level is at the rim of the glass. Carefully add pennies one at a time. How many pennies can you add to the full glass of water? What happens to the water level?

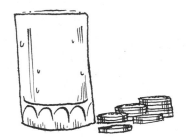

WHAT HAPPENED?

In water, molecules near the surface have a tendency to "cling" to each other, creating a stretchy skin called surface tension. The pennies you add take up space in the glass, causing the water to bulge up at the top. The surface tension stretches as much as possible, but finally breaks when there are just too many pennies in the glass.

GO WITH THE FLOW

Dazzle your friends with this amazing experiment in surface tension.

WHAT YOU'LL NEED

• **glass pint jar** • **cotton handkerchief** • **rubber band** • **water** • **bowl**

DIRECTIONS

1 Cover the jar with the handkerchief. Push the handkerchief down into the jar slightly to create a well, then secure it with a rubber band.

2 Add water to the jar through the handkerchief.

3 Pull the edges of the handkerchief down so that it is tight across the top of the jar. Quickly turn the jar upside down over a bowl. If the handkerchief is tight and you turn the jar quickly, the water will not spill.

4 While you are still holding the jar upside down, run your finger across the handkerchief. What happens?

WHAT HAPPENED?

The stretchy skin that forms near the surface of water, known as surface tension, helps keep the water from flowing out through the many tiny openings in the handkerchief. When you run your finger across the handkerchief, you break the surface tension and water pours out through the handkerchief.

THE WATER HOLE

Cohesion and adhesion sound a lot alike, but in this experiment you will see that they are actually quite different.

WHAT YOU'LL NEED

• spoon • food coloring, any color • ½ cup water • shallow dish
• eyedropper • rubbing alcohol

DIRECTIONS

❶ With the spoon, mix a few drops of food coloring into the water. Pour just enough colored water into the dish to cover the bottom.

❷ Use the eyedropper to place 1 drop of rubbing alcohol in the center of the colored water.

WHAT HAPPENED?

Cohesion is the tendency of a substance to cling to itself. Adhesion is the tendency of a substance to cling to other things. Water is cohesive, so it has a tendency to cling to itself. It will not adhere to the rubbing alcohol. Instead, the water pulls away from the alcohol, forming a ring around it.

Something Extra

For another example of cohesion, use a straw to place droplets of water on a sheet of waxed paper. Use a toothpick to move the droplets around on the paper. They will not lose their shape. Try pulling one drop close to another, then see what happens.

A REMARKABLE
RACE

Get ready to race with this unusual form of power, created when detergent disrupts the surface tension of water.

WHAT YOU'LL NEED

• **large bowl** • **water** • **scissors** • **piece of lightweight cardboard** • **dishwashing liquid**

DIRECTIONS

❶ Fill the bowl nearly to the rim with water.

❷ Cut a small triangle from the cardboard, about 1 inch wide on each side. Cut out a small notch on one side of the triangle. This is your "boat."

❸ Gently lay the boat flat on the surface of the water. The notch should be near the edge of the bowl.

❹ Carefully place a drop of dishwashing liquid in the water where the notch is. Watch the boat take off!

WHAT HAPPENED?

The molecules of the dishwashing liquid are attracted to the molecules of the water. This attraction disrupts the cohesion of the water molecules. When you place the drop of dishwashing liquid on the water, it breaks the surface tension, causing a ripple effect that forces the boat forward.

Something Extra

Another simple way to see the effect of dishwashing liquid on surface tension is to sprinkle pepper over the surface of a bowl of water. Place a drop of dishwashing liquid in the center of the bowl and watch the pepper move away from the center and toward the edge of the bowl.

ON THE RISE

How can a piece of cloth soak up so much water? That's capillary action at work. See for yourself.

WHAT YOU'LL NEED

• newspaper • small bowl • water • food coloring, any color • spoon • white cotton handkerchief

DIRECTIONS

❶ Spread a sheet of newspaper on a flat surface.

❷ Fill the bowl halfway with water, then place it on top of the newspaper. Add 6 drops of food coloring and stir with the spoon.

❸ Roll the handkerchief tightly into a tube. Place 2 inches of one end of the handkerchief in the colored water. Let the rest hang over the side of the bowl onto the newspaper.

❹ After 15 minutes, remove the handkerchief from the water and unroll it to see how much of it is wet. The food coloring will make it easier to tell.

WHAT HAPPENED?

Cloth absorbs, or soaks up, water through a process called capillary action. The tiny fibers of the cloth have small spaces in between them. Water molecules move through the spaces by adhering to the fibers. As the water molecules move farther up the handkerchief, they attract and draw up other water molecules below.

R O C K E T S AWAY!

Three hundred years ago Sir Isaac Newton figured out how and why things move. Get set to blast off with one of Newton's Laws of Motion.

WHAT YOU'LL NEED

• 11 feet of plastic fishing line • plastic drinking straw • oblong-shaped balloon • paper clip • tape

DIRECTIONS

1 Slip one end of the fishing line through the drinking straw. Find a place where you can stretch the fishing line at least 10 feet and tie each end to something secure. Attach both ends of the line, making sure that the line is taut.

2 Blow up the balloon and secure the end with the paper clip.

3 Tape the balloon rocket to the straw as shown.

4 Position the balloon at the beginning of the line. Remove the paper clip to release the rocket.

WHAT HAPPENED?

Newton's Third Law of Motion states that every action has an equal and opposite reaction. When you remove the paper clip, the air escapes from the balloon in one direction. This action produces a reaction: The balloon moves forward in the opposite direction.

HURRY UP

AND WEIGHT

Are things lighter or heavier in water? This experiment with buoyancy will help you find out.

WHAT YOU'LL NEED
• three pieces of lightweight string, each 8 inches long • pencil
• two large metal nuts • desk lamp or other object to hang string from
• two small drinking glasses • pitcher • water

DIRECTIONS

❶ Tie one end of the first piece of string to one end of the pencil. Tie one end of the second piece of string to the other end of the pencil.

❷ Tie one metal nut to the dangling end of each piece of string.

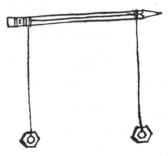

❸ Tie one end of the third piece of string around the middle of the pencil. Tie the other end to a desk lamp or other object so that the pencil hangs over a flat surface. The nuts should be suspended about an inch above the surface.

4 Arrange the glasses on the surface so that one nut hangs inside each glass. If you need to, adjust the pencil to make the nuts even with each other.

5 Fill one glass with water. The pencil will tilt.

WHAT HAPPENED?

In the air, the metal nuts are level because they weigh the same. In other words, the downward force of gravity is acting equally on each nut. When you add water to one glass, the nut inside is acted on by an upward force called buoyancy (the force that makes things float in water), which in effect makes the nut lighter. The pencil tilts down on the side that has more weight.

A DROP IN THE BUCKET

This cool trick may seem like magic, but it is really a demonstration of inertia.

WHAT YOU'LL NEED
• **3- by 5-inch index card** • **small drinking glass** • **nickel**

DIRECTIONS

1 Place the index card over the top of the glass.

2 Place the nickel in the middle of the card so that it is centered over the top of the glass.

3 Tuck the tip of your index finger behind your thumb, then flick your index finger against the edge of the card. The card will move forward and the coin will drop into the glass.

WHAT HAPPENED?

This is a demonstration of Newton's First Law of Motion regarding **inertia**. The card and coin are at rest and stay that way until acted on by a force. Your finger provides the force to move the card, but it does not act on the coin, so the coin stays behind. It falls into the glass because the card is no longer there to support it.

S P I N N I N G
E G G S

Sometimes it's hard to tell whether or not an egg is hard-boiled. Here's a surefire way to figure it out using inertia.

WHAT YOU'LL NEED
• **hard-boiled egg • raw egg**

DIRECTIONS

❶ Place both eggs on a hard, flat surface.

❷ Spin the hard-boiled egg with your hand. Place your finger on it for just a second to stop it from spinning.

❸ Now spin the raw egg. Place your finger on it for just a second to stop it from spinning. Do you notice any difference between the two eggs?

WHAT HAPPENED?

Newton's First Law of Motion explains the concept of inertia, which is the tendency of a body at rest, or a body in motion, to continue that way unless it is acted on by a force. (It is hard to believe, but a ball thrown up in the air would continue to move away from Earth if the force of gravity did not stop it and bring it back down.)

In this experiment the force of your finger on the hard-boiled egg is enough to stop it from spinning. The hard-boiled egg is solid, so the force acts on the egg as a whole. Although you exert roughly the same amount of force on the raw egg, it still spins slightly after you touch it. That is because the force acts on the hard shell, but not directly on the liquid inside the raw egg. The liquid continues to move slowly for another minute or two due to inertia.

FIELDS OF FORCE

Every magnet has an invisible field of force around it. Try this experiment to see what the magnetic field looks like.

WHAT YOU'LL NEED

• old scissors • new, soapless steel wool pad
• two bar magnets with north and south poles marked • sheet of plain paper

DIRECTIONS

❶ Carefully cut the steel wool into tiny pieces.

❷ Place one magnet on a table and hold the paper about ½ inch above it. With your free hand, sprinkle the steel wool bits on top of the paper. Shake the paper a little, then hold it still. A pattern will start to form.

❸ Move the paper away from the magnet and shake it again. Does the pattern disappear?

4 Now place the two magnets side by side with an inch of space between them. Set up the magnets as opposites of each other so there is a north and south pole at each end. Hold the paper with the steel wool pieces over the magnets. How does the pattern look this time? Turn one magnet around so that both north poles are at the same end, then hold the paper over both magnets again.

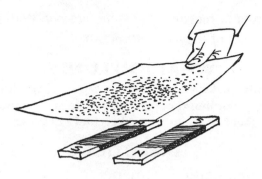

WHAT HAPPENED?

The steel wool bits on the paper are attracted to the lines of force, or the magnetic field, around the magnet. The pattern you see is the shape of the magnetic field. When you change the position of the magnets in step 4, the pattern of the magnetic field changes, too.

Something Extra

Try step 2 of this experiment holding the paper 2 to 3 inches above the magnet. How high does the magnetic field reach?

HOW
ATTRACTIVE

Some objects are attracted to magnets and some are not. With this experiment you will learn more about the power of magnetic attraction.

WHAT YOU'LL NEED

• **wooden ruler** • **plastic bottle cap** • **paper clips** • **coins**
• **aluminum cookie sheet** • **nails** • **magnet**
• **sheet of paper** • **handkerchief** • **drinking glass**

DIRECTIONS

❶ Spread out the ruler, bottle cap, paper clips, coins, cookie sheet, and nails on a flat surface.

❷ Try to pick up each of the materials with the magnet one at a time. Make a pile of the things that are attracted to the magnet.

❸ Now try to block the magnetic attraction. Put a sheet of paper between the magnet and an object. Does it block the magnetic effect? Next, see if the handkerchief can block the attraction. Can the drinking glass interfere with magnetic attraction?

WHAT HAPPENED?

A magnetic field is the area around a magnet in which the magnetic force can be felt. Magnets attract objects made of iron or steel. That is why the magnet was attracted to the nails and paper clips. The magnetic field is strong enough to penetrate some materials, but not others. As you can see, the magnet works through paper and cloth, but its effect weakens slightly through glass.

Something Extra

You can create a magnet out of a nail. Rub an iron or steel nail in one direction on a bar magnet about 30 times, then try to pick up a paper clip. By rubbing the nail across the magnet, you are aligning the molecules in the nail so that it acts temporarily as a magnet. See how long the magnetic effect will last.

THE GREAT
ATTRACTOR

Magnetic attraction can create some remarkable effects. This one will amaze you!

WHAT YOU'LL NEED

• drinking glass • long bar magnet • piece of thread, 10 inches long
• paper clip • tape

DIRECTIONS

❶ Set the glass upside down on a table. Place the bar magnet across the top of it so that it extends at least an inch over the edge of the glass.

❷ Tie one end of the thread to the paper clip. Touch the other end of the paper clip lightly to the bottom of the magnet so that the paper clip hangs from it.

❸ Pull down on the thread very gently so that the paper clip is still attracted to the magnet but there is space between them. It may take a few attempts to get this right.

❹ Without changing the position of the paper clip, tape the thread to the table. The paper clip will appear to defy gravity.

WHAT HAPPENED?

The magnetic force acts on the paper clip to pull it up. You exert another force on the paper clip by pulling the string down. When the two forces are equal, the paper clip appears to float in the air.

NORTH AND SOUTH

Some objects are naturally magnetic, but magnets can be created, too. Here's how.

WHAT YOU'LL NEED

**• steel sewing needle • bar magnet • clean plastic margarine container
• water • dishwashing liquid • thin slice of cork • tape (optional)**

DIRECTIONS

1 Rub the needle across the bar magnet at least 30 times in one direction.

2 Fill the container with water and place a drop of dishwashing liquid in the center.

3 Put the cork on top of the dishwashing liquid, then place the needle in the middle of the cork (tape the needle if it keeps rolling off). Spin the cork gently with your finger. When the cork stops, the ends of the needle will point north and south.

WHAT HAPPENED?

Nonmagnetic iron or steel is made up of tiny units that have their own north and south poles. The units are jumbled up so the poles face in different directions. If something causes the units to line up with all the poles facing in the same direction, the iron or steel becomes magnetized. When you rub the needle with the bar magnet in this experiment, you line up all the poles in the steel. The needle becomes magnetized and points north.

PUSH ME
PULL YOU

This experiment is positively electrifying! You'll learn how to create static electricity by manipulating a property called charge.

WHAT YOU'LL NEED
• **two balloons** • **two pieces of string, each 1 foot long** • **wool sweater or scarf**

DIRECTIONS

❶ Blow up both balloons and tie off each end with a knot. Attach one piece of string to each balloon.

❷ Hold the balloons by the strings and touch them together. What happens?

❸ Now rub the balloons on the sweater or scarf. Hold the balloons by the strings and touch them together again. What happens this time?

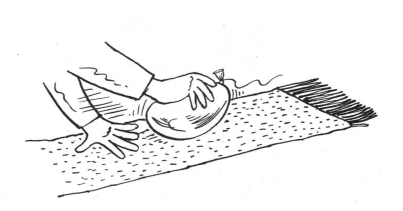

WHAT HAPPENED?

Atoms are made up of very tiny particles. Some of these particles, protons and electrons, have a property called charge. Protons have a positive charge, and electrons have a negative charge. Charges that are the same push each other away, and charges that are different attract each other. All atoms have equal numbers of particles so the charges cancel each other out. When you first touch the balloons together, their atoms have equal numbers of protons and electrons so they cancel each other out. The balloons are neutral to each other. By rubbing the balloons on the sweater or scarf, you "knock" electrons off the atoms in the wool. The electrons "stick" to atoms in the balloons, causing them to become negatively charged. Since both balloons are negatively charged, they repel, or push each other away.

Something Extra

What happens if you repeat the experiment but rub only one balloon on the wool? Try it and see.

L I G H T N I N G

S T R I K E S

Have you ever walked across a carpet, then gotten a shock when you touched something? That's static electricity at work.

WHAT YOU'LL NEED

• **large plastic bag** • **lightweight tin baking sheet** • **small metal object, such as a key**
• **wood table** • **baseball-sized piece of clay**

DIRECTIONS

❶ Place the plastic bag, baking sheet, and metal object on a wood tabletop.

❷ Press the clay into the center of the sheet so that it sticks to it. Grasp the clay and rub the bottom of the sheet back and forth on top of the plastic bag for a minute or two. Do not touch any part of the sheet while you are doing this.

❸ Turn off all the lights in the room to make it easier to see the spark. Using the clay as a handle, pick up the sheet and hold it near the metal object on the table. A small spark should jump from the sheet to the metal object.

WHAT HAPPENED?

Static electricity is a buildup of charge on the surface of an object. By rubbing the plastic bag, you cause static electricity to build up on the baking sheet. The wooden table and the clay do not attract static electricity, but the key does. Because the key and the tray have unlike charges, the static electricity on the tray jumps to the key. You see this transfer as a spark.

Something Extra

For more fun with static electricity, cut out 10 small paper butterflies. Rub a wool scarf across a hard rubber comb, then pass the comb over the butterflies without touching them. Watch the butterflies flutter. How long does the static electricity have an effect on the butterflies?

SPECIAL
....
SPOONS

Have you ever held a cup of hot cocoa on a cold day and felt your hands getting warmer? That feeling is the result of heat conduction.

WHAT YOU'LL NEED
• **butter, slightly softened**
• **three spoons, roughly the same size (one metal, one wood, one plastic)**
• **three small beads • cup, filled with hot water**

DIRECTIONS

1 Place a pea-sized dab of butter at the end of each spoon handle.

2 Push a bead into each dab of butter.

3 Place the spoons into the cup of hot water with the handles pointing up. Make sure that the handles do not touch each other. Which bead falls first?

WHAT HAPPENED?

When something is heated, its molecules begin to move faster. Moving molecules bump into other molecules, making them move, too. This process, called conduction, is one way heat energy spreads. Some materials are better conductors than others. For instance, metal is a good conductor. When you do this experiment, the heat from the water tends to move more quickly up the metal spoon, warming the butter and causing that bead to fall first.

A WET BLANKET

Can ice help to keep you warm? The answer may surprise you.

WHAT YOU'LL NEED

• **two pieces of aluminum foil** • **two outdoor thermometers**
• **paper towels** • **water** • **two saucers** • **freezer**

DIRECTIONS

❶ Fold the aluminum foil to make two loose pockets. Leave an opening at one end of each pocket so the thermometers can slip in and out.

❷ Put a thermometer in each pocket. Soak one of the paper towels with water, then wrap it around one foil pocket. Wrap a dry paper towel around the outside of the other pocket.

❸ Lay one pocket on each saucer. Place both in the freezer. Check the temperature of each thermometer every 5 minutes for 20 minutes. Does one stay warmer?

WHAT HAPPENED?

As water begins to freeze, it gives off energy in the form of heat. When the wet paper towel begins to freeze, it warms the air around the thermometer just a little, so the temperature is slightly higher than that on the other thermometer. Once the water on the paper towel has frozen, the air begins to cool again.

KEEPING
COOL

How do the brakes on a bicycle work? It's the force of friction. Here's more about it.

WHAT YOU'LL NEED
• **two dry blocks of wood, approximately 1 by 2 by 3 inches**
• **dry bar of soap**

DIRECTIONS

❶ Hold one block of wood in each hand. Rub the blocks together for about a minute. Stop rubbing and feel the surfaces that you rubbed together.

❷ Press the dry bar of soap on each block. You may have to press hard to coat the surfaces with soap. Rub the blocks together again. Does it feel different this time?

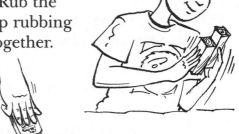

WHAT HAPPENED?

Most surfaces are slightly rough and will not slide past another surface easily. *Friction* is the term for this resistance. It takes energy to overcome friction and make materials slide past each other. A lot of that energy is converted to heat. You can feel that heat after you rub the blocks of dry wood together. When you add soap, the surfaces do not get as warm. Soap is a lubricant, which makes the surfaces slippery and allows the objects to slide past each other more easily.

Something Extra

Rub two metal lids together. Do the rubbed surfaces heat up? Smear cooking oil on the lids, then rub them together again. Do they heat up as much?

TIP THE
SCALE

You may not be able to see the air around you, but like all other matter, it takes up space and has weight. Here's how to prove it.

WHAT YOU'LL NEED

• three pieces of string, each 12 inches long • ruler • wire hanger
• two large balloons • sharp pin or needle

DIRECTIONS

❶ Tie one end of a piece of string to the center of the ruler at the 6-inch mark. Tie the other end to a hanger so the ruler hangs horizontally below it.

❷ Find a place to put the hanger, such as on the clothing rod inside a closet. Blow up both balloons to the same size. Attach the remaining strings to the balloons as shown. Tie one balloon to the ruler at the 1-inch mark and tie the other at the 11-inch mark. Adjust the strings to make the ruler level and the balloons balanced.

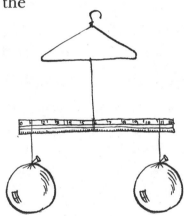

❸ Burst one balloon with the pin or needle.

WHAT HAPPENED?

Matter is any physical thing that takes up space and has weight. The air around us is made up of matter. When you blow up the balloons, you show that air takes up space. You also show that air has weight with this experiment. When you hang the two air-filled balloons from the ruler, it is balanced because they weigh the same. When you burst one balloon, the air escapes. The popped balloon does not weigh as much as the unpopped balloon. The weight of the air in the unpopped balloon pulls that side of the ruler down.

HEAVY
AIR

The weight of the atmosphere pressing down on the earth is known as air pressure. Try this experiment to feel the force of air pressure firsthand.

WHAT YOU'LL NEED
• **full sheet of newspaper** • **table** • **ruler**

DIRECTIONS

1 Spread the sheet of newspaper so that one edge of the paper runs along an edge of the table. Smooth it down so that it is flat.

2 Slip the ruler under the center of the newspaper so that it is sticking out about 3 inches over the edge of the table.

3 With your hand, slap the exposed end of the ruler. What happens?

4 Set up the newspaper and ruler again. This time, press your hand down on the ruler slowly. Now what happens?

WHAT HAPPENED?

It is very hard to lift the paper off the table by slapping on the ruler because air pressure is pushing down on the newspaper and holding it in place. When you press on the ruler slowly, air gets underneath the paper and equalizes the pressure. The newspaper moves easily.

POKEY
POTATO

Impress your friends by demonstrating the power of air pressure with this experiment.

WHAT YOU'LL NEED
• **raw potato** • **two plastic drinking straws**

DIRECTIONS

1 Place the potato on a hard surface, such as a table. Hold the first straw vertically a few inches above the potato, so that neither opening is covered.

2 Holding the potato in place with one hand, try to stab it with the straw. The straw will crumple and have little effect on the potato.

3 Hold the second straw vertically a few inches above the potato. This time, cover the top opening with your thumb.

4 Try to stab the potato again. What happens?

WHAT HAPPENED?

Compressed air is air that is squeezed into a small space, such as a straw. Compressed air provides a lot of force because it is more dense and is under greater pressure than the air outside the straw. The air trapped inside the second straw made the straw strong enough to actually stab the potato.

BREATHLESS

Can you and a friend stand in the same spot at the same time? One of the properties of matter is that no two things can share the same space at the same time.

WHAT YOU'LL NEED

• balloon • empty 2-liter soda bottle with no cap

DIRECTIONS

❶ Push most of the balloon down into the bottle, then stretch the neck of the balloon back over the opening of the bottle.

❷ Try to blow up the balloon by blowing air into the mouth of the bottle.

WHAT HAPPENED?

The balloon will not inflate because the bottle is already full of air. Air is made up of matter, so two volumes, or quantities, of air cannot occupy the same space at the same time. The air that is already in the bottle has nowhere else to go because the balloon is blocking the opening. Consequently, no new air can be added because there is no room for it.

U P
YOU GO

From birds to airplanes, things that fly rely on lift to escape the bonds of Earth's surface.

WHAT YOU'LL NEED
• scissors • notebook paper

DIRECTIONS

1 Cut a strip of notebook paper about 2 inches wide and 8 inches long.

2 Hold the paper horizontally in front of you with one of the ends near your mouth, nearly touching your lower lip. It will naturally curve downward.

3 Take a deep breath, then blow steadily over the strip. What happens to the loose end?

WHAT HAPPENED?

As you blow over the paper, the air above it starts to move faster than the air below it. The air molecules moving across the top of the paper spread out, and the air becomes thinner. This means that the air pressure above the paper is less than the air pressure below it. The slower, denser air below pushes upward and the paper rises. This is called lift.

S H I N·E

....

O N

When you look at the Moon, you're seeing not moonlight, but the reflected light of the Sun. Here's how it works.

WHAT YOU'LL NEED
• **fist-sized ball of clay** • **table that is in a corner**
• **hand mirror** • **flashlight**

DIRECTIONS

❶ Place the clay on the tabletop. Press the handle of the mirror into the clay so that it stands up facing you.

❷ Darken the room by turning off all the lights and closing any curtains or blinds. Stand at a slight angle to the left or right of the mirror.

❸ Turn on the flashlight and direct the beam of light at the mirror. A circle of light will appear on the wall next to the table.

WHAT HAPPENED?

The light from the flashlight is reflected off the surface of the mirror and onto the wall. If you aim the flashlight straight into the mirror, the light is reflected straight back at you. When you aim the flashlight at the mirror from an angle, the light bounces off the mirror at the same angle and hits the wall.

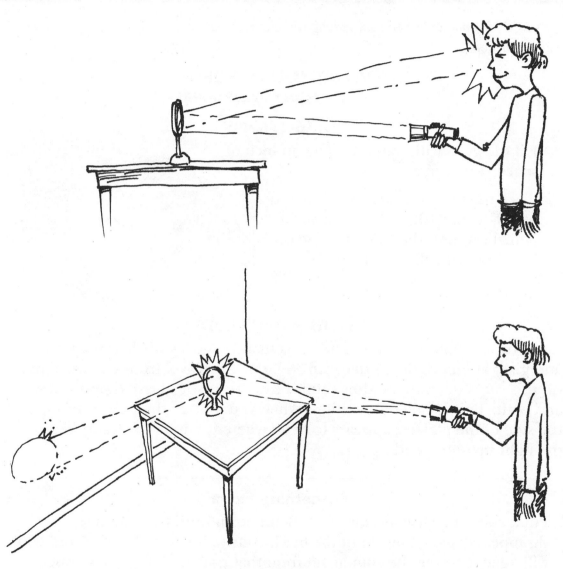

B E N D I N G

L I G H T

Do you think you could bend something without even touching it? Try this experiment with refraction.

WHAT YOU'LL NEED
• **drinking glass** • **water** • **pencil**

DIRECTIONS

1 Fill the glass with water, leaving an inch of space at the top.

2 Place the pencil inside the glass and lean it against the side. Look at the pencil through the side of the glass. Is the pencil still straight?

WHAT HAPPENED?

Light travels slower in water and glass than it does in air because water and glass are more dense than air. As light rays travel from one medium (in this case, air) into another (in this case, water or glass), they are slowed and bent. This is called refraction. When you look at the pencil through the side of the glass, it appears to bend where it enters the water because the light rays are bending.

Something Extra

Put a coin in a clear plastic bowl. Bend down until the coin just disappears below the rim of the bowl. Pour water into the bowl and you will be able to see the coin again from that position. Things in water appear closer than they really are because of refraction. This makes it difficult to judge distance in water.

THE COLOR OF LIGHT

Here's a way to create your own rainbow and get a picture-perfect glimpse of the visible spectrum.

WHAT YOU'LL NEED

• scissors • 3- by 5-inch index card • tape • tall drinking glass • water • 8½- by 11-inch sheet of white paper

DIRECTIONS

❶ Cut a 1- by 3-inch rectangle from the center of the 3- by 5-inch card.

❷ Tape the card lengthwise to the glass so the opening is directly over the rim. The rim of the glass should be in the center of the opening.

❸ Fill the glass to the rim with water and set it on a flat surface in front of a sunny window. Sunlight should shine through the glass via the hole in the card.

❹ Place a sheet of white paper on the floor in front of the glass. A rainbow will appear on the paper as the sunlight shines through the water.

WHAT HAPPENED?

A beam of light is actually made up of seven colors that the brain perceives as one. Each color in the beam vibrates at a different speed. When sunlight passes through water, each of the colors in the light is slowed and bent to a different extent. This produces a colorful arc known as a rainbow. The colors that vibrate faster are bent more than those that vibrate slower. Violet vibrates the fastest, so it is found on the inside of the arch. Red vibrates the slowest, so it is the outermost color.

SEEING

SOUND

Use this experiment to see something that is usually invisible—sound waves.

WHAT YOU'LL NEED

• **coffee can, both ends removed** • **plastic wrap** • **large rubber band**
• **I tablespoon sugar** • **small metal pan** • **metal spoon**

DIRECTIONS

❶ Set the coffee can on a flat surface. Place a piece of plastic wrap over the top of the coffee can. Secure the plastic wrap with the rubber band.

❷ Sprinkle the sugar on top of the plastic wrap.

❸ Hold the metal pan within an inch of the side of the can. They should not be touching. With your free hand, bang hard on the side of the pan with the spoon. The sugar particles will jump.

WHAT HAPPENED?

When you bang on the pan with a spoon, you cause the nearby air molecules to vibrate. This vibration passes through other air molecules in waves, called sound waves. When these waves of vibrations enter your ear, your brain interprets them as sound. In this experiment you cannot see the waves, but they are what make the tiny grains of sugar bounce on the plastic wrap.

Something Extra

Try using other sources of sound in this experiment. For example, blow a whistle, yell, or sing into the side of the can. Will it make a difference in how high the sugar particles jump?

HEARING THINGS

Here's a way to transfer sound waves to your ears by the spoonful.

WHAT YOU'LL NEED

• **2 feet of lightweight cotton string** • **metal spoon** • **table**

DIRECTIONS

1 Tie the center of the string around the handle of the spoon.

2 Wrap one end of the string around each index finger. Place the tips of your index fingers in your ears.

3 Lean forward so that the spoon taps against a table. In your ears it will sound like a bell ringing.

WHAT HAPPENED?

Sound is actually just waves of vibrations. When the vibrations reach your ear, your brain perceives the vibrations as sound. Sound vibrations travel more easily through solids than they do through air. Sound waves that reach your ear through a solid are stronger than those that are traveling in different directions through the air. By striking the metal spoon against the table, you start the vibration, which travels directly up the string—a solid—and into your ears.

FREE FALL

Is the force of gravity stronger with bigger objects? You may want to ask a friend to help you find out.

WHAT YOU'LL NEED

• tennis ball • marble • crumpled ball of aluminum foil
• baseball • 2-inch-square block of wood

DIRECTIONS

❶ Stand up straight and hold one of the five test objects listed above in each hand. Be sure to hold them at the same distance from the floor.

❷ Let go of the objects at exactly the same time and watch them drop. Do they hit the floor at the same time? You may want to ask a friend to observe from floor level.

❸ Repeat the experiment several times using a different pair of objects each time.

WHAT HAPPENED?

Earth's gravity causes objects to fall toward the center of the planet. The ground, however, stops the fall. The force of gravity on the objects you tested is equal, no matter how big or how heavy they are. Consequently, they fall at the same rate.

Something Extra

Try this with a tennis ball and a sheet of paper. Do they hit the floor at the same time? Crumple the paper into a ball and try it again. Although the force of gravity on both objects is equal, the flat paper you used in the first test falls more slowly because of its shape. The air slows down light, flat objects. The Moon has gravity but no air, so a ball and a sheet of paper would fall at exactly the same rate on the Moon.

STANDING
....
TALL

Everybody has a center of gravity. Try this demonstration and you will see how important it is.

WHAT YOU'LL NEED
• handkerchief

DIRECTIONS

❶ Stand with your feet slightly apart in the middle of a room. Drop the handkerchief in front of your feet, then bend over and pick it up.

❷ Now stand with your back against a wall. Drop the handkerchief in front of you, then try to bend over and pick it up. What happens to your balance?

WHAT HAPPENED?

You have a center of gravity, or an innate sense that helps you stay balanced without even having to think about it. As you move, your muscles are constantly making adjustments to keep you balanced. When you bend over, your body makes dozens of automatic adjustments, such as leaning back slightly or shifting your hips. When your back is against a wall, your body can't make these adjustments. You can't pick up the handkerchief this way without losing your balance.

Something Extra

Stand with your right side against a wall. Be sure the side of your right foot is touching the wall. Try to raise your left leg out to the side.

BALANCING ACT

If you like a challenge, this experiment with the center of gravity is for you. You can really amaze your friends when you learn how to do it, but you will need an adult to help you.

WHAT YOU'LL NEED
• knife • potato • new pencil, sharpened • empty 2-liter soda bottle with cap
• two metal forks of equal size

DIRECTIONS

❶ Ask an adult to help you cut a 1-inch-thick slice from the center of the potato. Push the pencil through the center.

❷ Place the capped bottle on a flat surface. Try to balance the pencil (on its eraser) on top of the cap. Will it work?

❸ Stick the two forks into opposite sides of the potato.

❹ Now try balancing the pencil (on its eraser) again on top of the soda bottle. You may have to adjust the forks slightly.

WHAT HAPPENED?

All things have a balance point, or center of gravity, at which they are in perfect balance. The pencil with the potato is top heavy and will not balance. By adding forks to the potato, you change the center of gravity. With a little work, you can make it balance.

ROLLING
UP

This experiment seems to defy gravity, but it's just another example of how the center of gravity works.

WHAT YOU'LL NEED
• two plastic funnels • masking tape
• three books (each 1 inch thick) • two yardsticks

DIRECTIONS

1 Hold the wide ends of the two funnels together. Secure them with masking tape.

2 Stack two books on the floor. Place the third book 30 inches in front of the stack.

3 Place the end of each yardstick on opposite sides of the taller stack. Rest the other ends of the yardsticks side by side, with the ends touching, on the single book. The yardsticks will form a *V* shape.

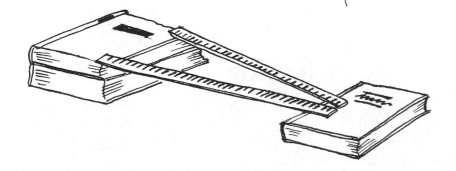

4 Place the funnels at the bottom of the yardsticks so that the taped part of the funnels is at the center of the *V*. They will appear to roll uphill.

WHAT HAPPENED?

As the funnels begin to roll, they are actually slipping lower in the widening track. At the beginning of the track where it is narrow, the center of the funnels is resting next to the yardsticks. As the track opens up, the funnels slip lower and lower until the ends are resting next to the yardsticks. The center of gravity of the funnels shifts downward, and the funnels appear to roll up the *V* track.

S O G G Y
S O I L

Some types of soil hold, or retain, water and some don't. Try this experiment in water retention to determine which types of soil are best for retaining water.

WHAT YOU'LL NEED
• **pencil** • **two paper cups** • **½ cup sandy soil**
• **½ cup clay soil** • **two measuring cups** • **I cup water**

DIRECTIONS

1 With the pencil, make a hole in the bottom of each paper cup. Fill one paper cup with sandy soil and the other with clay soil.

2 Hold the cup with clay soil over an empty measuring cup. Pour ½ cup water into the clay soil–filled cup. Measure how much water drains through in two minutes.

3 Now hold the cup with sandy soil over another measuring cup. Pour ½ cup water into the sandy soil–filled cup. Measure how much water drains through in two minutes.

WHAT HAPPENED?

There are many different kinds of soil. Soil is formed from weathered rocks and minerals. Its texture is influenced by the climate and plants in the area. Clay soil has a fine texture, with few air spaces between the grains. It holds water well. Sandy soil has a coarse texture, with many air spaces between the grains, which allows water to drain through it easily.

BUBBLING ROCK

If you are a rock collector, this experiment is perfect for you! Use this procedure to determine the carbonate content in rock.

WHAT YOU'LL NEED

• collection of rocks • water • metal nail file • eyedropper • white vinegar

DIRECTIONS

1 If you don't already have a collection, gather a few rocks from outside. Try to find a variety by looking in different areas. Rinse the rocks in plain water and dry them.

2 Make a slightly rough patch on each rock by rubbing the surface with a metal nail file.

3 With the eyedropper, place 1 drop of vinegar on the rough patch of each rock. Observe the reaction on each rock.

WHAT HAPPENED?

Certain rocks are made up of the remains of tiny shelled sea creatures called carbonates. When carbonates come in contact with a weak acid such as vinegar, it creates a chemical reaction that produces carbon dioxide gas. If you see a little bubbling when you test a rock, then it probably contains carbonates. Other rocks should not have any reaction to the vinegar.

WASHING AWAY

Erosion is the wearing away of rocks and soil by water. In this experiment you will test how plants affect the erosion process.

WHAT YOU'LL NEED

• **three shallow baking pans** • **2 cups pebbles** • **2 cups soil**
• **newspaper** • **four books (each about 1 inch thick)** • **leaves, twigs, and grass**
• **2 cups water** • **colander**

DIRECTIONS

1 Fill two baking pans with pebbles, then cover the pebbles with soil.

2 Place the third baking pan on a flat surface covered with newspaper. Stack two books at each end of the pan. Lean the two soil-filled pans against the books so they tilt downward into the third pan.

3 In one of the soil-filled pans, cover the soil completely with a layer of leaves, twigs, and grass.

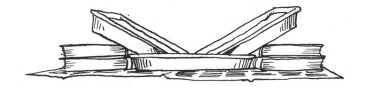

4 Pour 1 cup water through the colander into the pan with the leafy layer. Observe what happens.

5 Pour 1 cup water through the colander into the pan with just soil and pebbles. What happens this time?

WHAT HAPPENED?

Rainwater can quickly wash away unprotected soil because there is nothing to anchor it in place. Plants, grass, leaves, and twigs keep soil from eroding by shielding it and anchoring it in place. Much of the soil from the pan without the leafy layer is likely to have washed into the spillover pan.

DRIPS
AND DROPS

Water is unusual because it exists naturally in all three states of matter—solid, liquid, and gas. This experiment with condensation shows that water vapor is always in the air, even when you can't see it.

WHAT YOU'LL NEED
• **large glass jar with lid** • **ice cubes** • **water** • **towel**

DIRECTIONS

❶ Fill the jar nearly to the top with ice. Add a little water to the jar—the water level should be about an inch from the bottom.

❷ Fasten the lid tightly on the jar. Dry the outside of the jar with the towel.

❸ Place the jar in a warm spot that is not in direct sunlight. Wait 15 minutes.

WHAT HAPPENED?

Droplets of water, known as condensation, form on the outside of the jar. Condensation occurs when warm, moist air meets something cold. As the warm air cools, the molecules in the water vapor slow down and move closer together, changing the water that is in the air from a gas to a liquid.

THE PRESSURE

IS ON

Have you ever wondered how forecasters know when the weather is going to change? Follow these directions to make a barometer and do some forecasting of your own.

WHAT YOU'LL NEED

• scissors • balloon • large glass jar • large rubber band • plastic straw
• glue • 3- by 5-inch card • marker • tape

DIRECTIONS

❶ Cut a piece from the balloon that is large enough to stretch over the top of the jar. Secure it in place with the rubber band. Then cut a piece from the straw that is 6 inches long.

❷ Put a drop of glue in the center of the stretched balloon. Set one end of the straw on top of the glue so that it is lying horizontally. Place the jar on a flat surface near a wall.

❸ Holding the card lengthwise, write HIGH at the top of it and LOW at the bottom. Tape the card onto the wall next to the jar.

❹ Check the weather report (including air pressure) for your area every day for two weeks. Check your barometer each day. Monitor the barometer closely before, during, and after any storms. Record your results.

WHAT HAPPENED?

When air pressure is high, the air will push down on the balloon in your barometer, causing the straw to point to HIGH. When air pressure is low, the straw will point to LOW. High air pressure generally indicates clear weather ahead, while low air pressure indicates cloudy weather. Changes in air pressure usually mean the weather will be changing, so a barometer is very helpful when making predictions about the weather.

RED SKY
AT NIGHT

Why does the sky often appear red at sunset? It's because of scattered light in the atmosphere. Try this experiment to see how it works.

WHAT YOU'LL NEED

• water • large glass jar or clear plastic container • golf-ball-sized piece of clay
• flashlight • milk • spoon

DIRECTIONS

1 Pour water into the container until it is about three-quarters full. Place the container on a flat surface.

2 Press the clay onto the flat surface about 3 inches from the container. Press the flashlight down into the clay so that it stays in place and is pointed at the container.

3 Pour milk into the water until the container is almost full. Stir with a spoon. Wait for the mixture to become still, then shine the light through it. Observe the container from the side opposite the flashlight.

WHAT HAPPENED?

The light we see is made up of different colors that move at slightly different speeds. When the beam of light passes through the milk-and-water mixture, it strikes tiny particles that break the light up into different colors and scatter it. When you look at the container from the side opposite the flashlight, you see light rays that have been scattered. Therefore, you see only the longer, slower red light rays. A similar effect takes place when sunlight passes through the atmosphere. The sunlight hits particles in the atmosphere that break it up and scatter it. During the day, it is scattered a little and you see the sky as blue. At sunset, the sun is low on the horizon and must pass through more atmosphere. The light is scattered more. In fact, it is scattered so much that you don't see the faster rays, only the longer, slower red rays.

P E T
F O G

Fog is simply a ground-hugging cloud. Here's how to create your own fog in a bottle.

WHAT YOU'LL NEED
• **empty 2-liter soda bottle with no cap** • **very warm water** • **large ice cube**

DIRECTIONS

1 Fill the bottle with very warm water to heat the air inside. Let it sit for a minute.

2 Pour out all but an inch of the water.

3 Place the ice cube over the neck of the bottle so that it completely covers the opening.

WHAT HAPPENED?

The warm air inside the bottle contains water vapor. The water vapor cools when ice is placed on top of the bottle. It condenses into tiny droplets, which look much like fog.

Something Extra
Try this experiment again, but this time wrap the ice in plastic wrap.

R O U N D
A N D   R O U N D

Tornadoes are among the most destructive windstorms on Earth. Create a tornado in a bottle to demonstrate the funnel form of such storms. You may need a friend to help you.

WHAT YOU'LL NEED
• **marker** • **two empty 2-liter soda bottles with no caps**
• **water** • **food coloring or glitter** • **duct tape**

DIRECTIONS

1 Label the bottles #1 and #2. Fill bottle #1 about three-quarters full with water and add a few drops of food coloring or some glitter (or both).

2 You may need someone to help you with this step. Turn bottle #2 upside down over bottle #1. Secure the necks of the bottles together with duct tape.

3 Turn the bottles over so that #1 is on top. With a good grip on the joined bottlenecks, swirl the bottles in a circular motion. Set the bottles on a flat surface. A funnel of water should form as the water drains down into the bottom bottle.

WHAT HAPPENED?

A tornado is a very powerful whirling windstorm, which usually starts when warm air rises and cool air sinks, forming an area of unsettled air called a storm cell. Differences in wind speeds probably cause the air around the center of the storm cell to rotate. This creates a whirling funnel cloud. Once it hits the ground, it becomes a tornado. In this experiment you move the bottles in a circular motion to get the water spinning. It forms a funnel of water similar to the funnel of wind in a tornado.

WHICH
IS WHICH?

You might be surprised by the results of this experiment on the sensitivity of human touch.

WHAT YOU'LL NEED
• three small bowls • very warm water • very cold water
• water at room temperature

DIRECTIONS

❶ Fill one bowl with very warm water, one with very cold water, and the last with room-temperature water.

❷ Place one hand in the warm water and the other in the cold water for about 30 seconds.

❸ Now put both hands in the room-temperature water. The hand that was in the warm water will feel like it is in cold water, and the hand that was in the cold water will feel like it is in warm water.

WHAT HAPPENED?

Temperature is the measure of how hot or cold something is. The human body is not always accurate when judging temperature. In this experiment the feeling in each hand is influenced by the temperature of the water that it was in originally.

HOLD
YOUR BREATH

Take a deep breath. Can you guess how much air was in that breath? Try this test of lung capacity and see for yourself. This experiment works best with a friend to help, but it can be done alone.

WHAT YOU'LL NEED
• 1-gallon plastic milk bottle with no cap • large plastic tub or container
• water • straw with a flexible neck

DIRECTIONS

❶ Fill the bottle with water, then fill about three-quarters of the tub with water. Set the tub on a flat surface.

❷ Hold the bottle over the tub. Cover the mouth of the bottle and flip the bottle over. Put your hand and the neck of the bottle in the water-filled tub, then remove your hand from the mouth. Make sure the mouth of the bottle stays under water. Steady the bottle with your hands, or have a friend hold it for you.

❸ Bend the straw's flexible neck and insert the short end into the mouth of the bottle. Take a deep breath and blow into the straw.

WHAT HAPPENED?

The air from your lungs enters the inverted bottle and forces the water out. Your lungs hold a lot more air than is in the bottle, but you never breathe it all out at once.

PERFECT

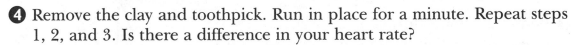

PULSE

Your heart pumps blood throughout your entire body. You can tell how many times it pumps each minute by taking your pulse.

WHAT YOU'LL NEED
• pea-sized ball of clay • toothpick

DIRECTIONS

❶ Place your hand palm side up on a flat surface. Press the ball of clay onto your wrist about an inch below the base of your thumb.

❷ Insert the toothpick into the clay so that it stands upright. Observe carefully as the toothpick twitches slightly back and forth. If it doesn't move, shift the clay until you see the toothpick twitch.

❸ Count the number of twitches that occur in 15 seconds, then multiply that number by four.

❹ Remove the clay and toothpick. Run in place for a minute. Repeat steps 1, 2, and 3. Is there a difference in your heart rate?

WHAT HAPPENED?

Your heart beats a certain number of times each minute. Everyone's heartbeat is different, but children average between 80 and 130 heartbeats per minute at rest. With each beat, your heart pumps blood throughout your body. You can feel your pulse as each wave of blood passes through the blood vessel located just below the skin of your wrist. This movement causes the toothpick on your wrist to twitch. Exercise raises the rate of your heartbeat. Your heart beats faster in order to pump blood to all of the hard-working muscles in your body. The toothpick on your wrist probably twitches more often after you exercise.

THE SEE-THROUGH HAND

You can't always believe what you see. Sometimes your eyes play tricks on you. These are known as optical illusions.

WHAT YOU'LL NEED
• sheet of construction paper • tape

DIRECTIONS

❶ Roll the paper into a tube big enough to look through comfortably with one eye. Tape the paper so that it will not unravel.

❷ Look through the tube with your right eye. Keep your left eye open and look straight ahead. Place your left hand against the far end of the tube, with the palm facing you. Move your hand slowly a few inches from the end of the tube. Stare straight ahead as you do this, not at your hand. What do you see?

WHAT HAPPENED?

Both of your eyes face forward, so your field of vision overlaps. This is called binocular vision. The brain tries to blend what each eye sees into one image. In this case, the left eye sees the hand and the right eye sees the hole. The brain perceives this as a hand with a hole in it.

Something Extra
Hold your index fingers in front of your eyes. Point your fingers at each other but leave an inch-wide gap between them. Keep both eyes open. After a minute you will see a tiny "fingertip" in between your real fingers.

M Y S T E R Y
M O O N

Sometimes the Moon looks larger when it appears at the horizon. Is it really larger, or is it an optical illusion? Here's a way to find out.

WHAT YOU'LL NEED

• flat piece of glass from a picture frame, with the edges taped for safety
(ask a parent to do this for you)
• marker or crayon

DIRECTIONS

❶ As the Moon appears just above the horizon, hold the glass at arm's length in front of you and trace its shape on the glass with the marker.

❷ After the Moon is high in the sky, hold the glass at arm's length again and look at the Moon. It will fit perfectly into the circle you drew earlier.

WHAT HAPPENED?

Although the Moon may appear larger near the horizon, it is just an optical illusion. Sometimes your brain judges the size of an object by the size of other, familiar objects around it. When the Moon is low, there are plenty of objects for your brain to compare it to, such as trees, houses, or hills. High up in the sky, there is nothing else to compare it to, so you perceive its size more accurately.